ATER VOTUM

A Book of Daemonolatry Prayer

ATER VOTUM

A Book of Daemonolatry Prayer

DB Publishing 2007

PRAYER

The following prayers were contributed by many Demonolaters and Theistic Satanists. We would like to thank all who contributed to this project. May you be blessed in Lucifer's name. Naamah.

Please Note: Amen is used in prayers herein. Amen, meaning "So be it" in Hebrew, has even earlier origins in prayer. In ancient Egypt Amen was the hidden aspect (and highest power) of Amen Ra. To send the prayer to the highest, most hidden aspect of deity, Amen was said at the end of prayer. For Satanists and Daemonolaters, you may end your prayer with Satan, Naamah, Lucifer, or simply Amen. It's really up to you.

Prayer for Financial Security

I ask of you, Lucifer, to grant me wisdom and aide in obtaining stability in material matters. In your name I invoke the strength of your nature to aide me. Lord Lucifer, hear my prayer.

I ask of you, Belial, to grant me stability in this tangible world that I may not want for material things. In your name I invoke the strength of your nature to aide me. Lord Belial, hear my prayer.

I ask of you, Belphegore, to help me obtain financial opportunity and victory that I may dwell in the flesh comfortably with the necessities I need. In your name I invoke the strength of your nature to aide me. Lord Belphegore, hear my prayer.

Amen.

Prayer for Victory in Legal Disputes or Judgments in Your Favor

Lord Leviathan, please bring judgment in my favor that I may come out of this dispute in victory. By Leviathan, may those who oppose me stumble and not stand in the way of my success. I pray for your help and mercy in your wise judgment. Amen.

Prayer for Emotional Strength (for women)

I am as Tezrian going into battle, and Sonnelion, in control of all before me. I am as Unsere, the wise matriarch, and Lilith, the High Priestess. In the names of Tezrian, Sonnelion, Unsere, and Lilith, I ask you grant me emotional strength to overcome my present obstacles and to emerge unscathed. Unsere, give me strength. Lilith, give me strength. Tezrian, give me strength. Sonnelion, give me strength. By Delepitore and the pillars of the sisters, rises the raging river above me. I am the creator, the sorceress, of all before me. I am. Amen.

Healing Prayer
By Catlovingdemon (OFS Forum)

Hail Verrine, full of green, the life is with thee, lively art thou amongst demons, and lively is the fruit of thy self, health. Happy Verrine, maker of health, dwell in your followers, now and each hour of our lives amen.

Rites of Belphegore Prayer

Lord Belphegore, accept this blood offering as my respect and devotion to your divine nature. I pray bless and keep myself and my loved ones in your divine power this coming year. By Belial, Baal, Balberith and the many Daemons of Earth, may we be blessed with your abundance. Naamah.

Prayer to Lucifer

It is our Lord Lucifer who hath brought us from the darkness into the light. He brightens our path so that we may find enlightenment. We honor him. His winds carry with them the promise of lessons learned for this lifetime. Hail Lucifer.

Prayer for Protection and Strength

Lord Satan, hear me. Blessed in your name I pray please keep us safe and help us find internal strength and resolve. Henceforth I vow my everlasting devotion and love. So be it.

Nine Prayers
by S. T. Dukante-Mallory

The Daemonic Creed: I believe in Satan, the Ether of All the Is, Creator of the universe and the spirit that binds the All together. I believe in and give my allegiance to Lucifer, the Enlightenment of Satan, who was conceived by Unsere in compassion and understanding of all things. I give myself to the infernal flames of Baphometic Fire that I am reborn as the Phoenix in Satan's name. Amen.

The Infernal Father: Our Infernal Father, who art in Hell, hallowed by Thy name. This is your kingdom here, on earth, as are all of the heavens. Give us your wisdom and your enlightenment. Teach us to cultivate knowledge and happiness. Let us know our fellow man. Lead us away from ignorance and toward truth. Amen.

The Third Prayer: Glory be to Satan. As it was in the beginning is now and ever shall be, All without end. Amen. Unsere, teach us to have mercy for our enemies. May Amducious teach us temperance in justice. Naamah.

The Hail Elementals: Hail Belial, bountiful earth, the Daemons of earth anoint thee king. Thou art abundance and prosperity among them all. Hail Lucifer, full of Light, the Daemons of air anoint thee king. Thou art enlightenment and wisdom among them all. Hail Flereous, Lord of Fire, the Daemons of fire anoint thee king. Thou art rebirth and passion and desire among them all. Hail Leviathan, the wise Serpent, the Daemons of water anoint thee king. Thou art justice and compassion among them.

The Fifth Prayer : Satan, please send us the one who brings us to the Daemonic Divine in Daath. By Lucifuge

Rofocale in union with Verrine and Amducious and all of creation binding the spirit to the physical realm, Amen.

The Balance of Life & Death: Hail to Unsere, mother of all creation, the source of all life. Hail to Eurynomous, father of souls, the protector of the dead. May together you hold the sacred balance of life and death and guide us on our journey through both the realms of the living and the dead. In Satan's holy and infernal name, Naamah.

Let Us Pray: O Satan, by the life of Unsere, death of Eurynomous and resurrection of Enlightenment through Lucifer, you balance us. We are enriched by the truth of the eternal cycle of life through Belial, Lucifer, Flereous, and Leviathan. We respect those powers of Verrine and healing and the Destruction of Amducious. We beseech the Demonic Divine that while meditation on these mysteries of the nine Divinities, we may learn to know ourselves and become stronger through you. Amen.

Satan's Prayer: Beloved Satan, I worship and adore You. I seek your infernal wisdom to guide me through this life and beyond. Amen.

The Ninth Prayer: Most Holy and Gracious, the Infernal divinities. We implore your protection along our paths. Blessed are our brethren who seek enlightenment within the Daemonic Divine. Hail to our infernal Brethren who walk in the path of Lucifer. Inspire us with confidence and bring us abundance and peace. Naamah.

Prayer for Peace

In the name of Unsere may we find understanding and through Lucifer may we discover the wisdom to find peace in Satan. In the Demons names we pray, may there be peace on every corner of the earth and within our homes and families that we may herald in a new generation with love and understanding. Naamah.

Prayer for Soldiers

Dear Amducius. Please watch over our soldiers that they may be safe from harm this night. May they be blessed with strength and resolve to perform their duties in the face of adversity. Protect our soldiers Amon, and Mammon, and Abaddon. Stand beside them upon the battle fields and guide them. Let them be victorious in battle and come home to us safe. In your names we pray. Amen.

Prayer for Loved Ones Far Away

Lord Satan bless and protect my loved one [insert name] who is away from me now. Please grant him/her the wisdom to stay safe and be happy and enjoy all that life has to offer. In Satan's name we pray. Amen.

Prayer for Mothers

By our Lady Unsere I pray for all mothers that they have the wisdom to guide their children and families and that they are blessed with patience and fortitude. Bless our mothers for they guide us and keep us together. Bless our mothers for they are the bringers of life. Amen.

Prayer for Fathers

By our Father Satan I pray for all fathers that they have the wisdom to guide their children and families and that they are blessed with strength and patience. Bless our fathers for they are our strength and protection. Bless our fathers for they help to sustain us in childhood. Amen.

Prayer for Children

In Unsere's name protect and keep our children that they may grow up to be functional members of society. Let them see Lucifer's wisdom and partake of all life has to offer. Blessed are the children. Amen.

Thanksgiving

By the Demons of Earth we give thanks for all we have to eat. The bounty that fills us and sustains us. We thank thee for that which nourishes our bodies and keeps us alive. In the names of Belial, Behemot, Belphegore, and Baal, Amen.

A Reflection Prayer
by Callie Matthews

Lord Lucifer, as I reflect on my past I give my thanks to you for all you have taught me. You showed me truth when I was lied to. You taught me to find strength in myself. You gave me wisdom in times of need. Through many times in my life you were there for me when I felt lost, alone, and weak. You lifted me up and made the light to shine down upon me, illuminating my path. Hail Lucifer. I give you my thanks, my love, and my eternal devotion. Amen.

Beginning to Understand
By Xophier

I hold in my hand all but nothing
For all I know to be true rests within my heart
Not within tomes of obscure riddles
Or sun baked men who ponder eternity

When the world tries to engulf me
I feel not a hand pulling
But rather one who pushes into the deluge
So I must make my stand

How do I describe the magnificent monsters of a child's
night terror
When unveiled and shown truth
Not many stand to ancient fears
But I am glad I had

Feelings like being rocked by the ocean
Shown by experiencing self flaws and faults
Understanding as well we are only human
And show us to push that title

Remembering when I took that stand on such a narrow cliff
Instead of walking where so many felt safe
I took the path and was cast aside for such
I thought about the past, but my pride would not let it cloud

While my legs could no longer carry me and my knees
buckled
I knew I had done something, at least for me the world
stopped for the second
Before I felt alone, I felt renewed as my legs began to move
At that time I thought for a second I heard a voice

The whistle of the wind through the trees
The lull of the mystical ocean
The crackle of fire
The nagging of the cicada?

And with time I know
That those sounds will be prophetic
To my pen and paper scribe
But now, I must understand myself

As I do this not so small task
But I have divine guidance
To understand myself
To understand, Satan

Mammon bring our Silver
By Catlovingdemon

Mammon bring our silver,
Belphegore our gold:
Bring us all the treasure
We can have or hold.

Belial, give both real diamonds
And the morning dew;
Give us shining sapphires
And skies of healing blue.

We'll not just have emeralds–
But leaves so new and green;
Roses match the rubies
In which we are seen.

Belial, who gave treasures
To your children small,
Teach us how to love them
And grow like them all.

Make us bright as silver:
Highly-prized as gold
Ashtaroth, like roses
Let friendships unfold

Gay as leaves in springtime,
Or straight as a pine–
Verrine, who's magic's healing,
Keep our bodies fine.

Elemental Prayer
By Catlovingdemon

Lucifer of hopefulness, Lucifer, joy,
Promethean vigour no cares could destroy,
Be there at our waking, and give us, we pray,
Your Sun in our hearts, Lucifer, at break of day.

Flereous of eagerness, Flereous, fire,
Your hand's skill fulfilling your will and your ire,
Be there at our labours, and give us, we pray,
Your skill in our hearts, Flereous, at noon of day.

Leviathan of kindness, Leviathan, grace,
Your waters swift to welcome, our blood to embrace,
Be there at our homing, and give us, we pray,
Your blessing in our hearts, Leviathan, at eve of day.

Belial of gentleness, Belial of pleasure,
Your voice rich and earthy, your presence is treasure,
Be there at our sleeping, and give us, we pray,
Your wealth in our hearts, Belial, at end of day.

Prayer for Satan
By Laura Naysmith

Father Satan, I call to you from the deepest parts of my heart, I praise your name with every breath of my body, I worship you with every fiber of my being. You've shown me what true strength is. You have shown me what true love is. Out of the darkness you came to show me the true light.

My master, my father
Amen

Tasa Satanachia
A Prayer
by lianna diabolique, Washington, DC 2006 (c)

Black Arts, Channel Satanachia, Lord of this age
Unleash, Come Forth and commune in fire and lust and
desire
My soul thy dwelling place, my flesh thy consummation
Thine will be done by and through me, infernal rage
Channeling and quintessence desirous a subconscious
Hunger of my consciousness
rage for thy desire of unspeakable ecstasy
To thee through Almighty Sathanas,
in complete obedience to you doth I smoke this herb
to ever more come under your spell
May these visions hallucinations for our mutual
gratification open my soul completely to you

Possession, my third eye open wide, my soul black
Indwell in this place as thy smoke dissolves within
And opens my soul wide
Zazas, Zazas, Nasatanda Zazas!!!!!!
Oh Devil of Hell I worship thee,
Goat of tens of billions of spawn
I desire thee, I love and adore thee

Judas thy desire come forth
Four Crowned Princes within me
Shub Niggurath
Lex Talionis
Enrage my blood, unleash
All Manner of Sin I delight
My Black Soul Embrace
Ganic Tasa Fubin Satanachia

Ganic Tasa Fubin Satanachia
Unleash this Fire
Commune
Pleasures of the Flesh
Vengeance and Lust
Submission and Blasphemy
I curse the light
Open Wide Your Gates of Majesty
Divine Presence Come Forth
Dread adversary, maketh heavens to shake
Come forth enraged

Tasa reme laris Satan
Tasa reme laris Satan
Tasa reme laris Satan
Tasa reme laris Satan
Tasa reme laris Satan
Tasa reme laris Satan
Blood flow of the Lion's Den
Flood Rivers and Lakes
Zazas, Zazas, Nasatanda Zazas!!!!!!
Semen of Mastery, Rape of Angels Rapture
Ejaculate of Chaos, orgasm of Undead Souls
Immortal Eros, darkness rich and warm
Come Forth and dwell in my baptized essence
Born Again of The Blasphemies
By the Blood Pact
Zazas, Zazas, Nasatanda Zazas!!!!!!
I am Born of the dragon, Harlot, with Unholy Spirit
Sodomize the Children of Abel that their pleasure gasps

Will enrage your Vengeance Divine
Oh Tasa reme laris Satan, my soul is Thine!!!!!!
Oh Tasa reme laris Satan, my soul is Thine!!!!!!
Oh Tasa reme laris Satan, my soul is Thine!!!!!!
Oh Tasa reme laris Satan, my soul is Thine!!!!!!

Oh Tasa reme laris Satan, my soul is Thine!!!!!!
Oh Tasa reme laris Satan, my soul is Thine!!!!!!
Zazas, Zazas, Nasatanda Zazas!!!!!!

This Chambre that thou hast blessed
Spawn of thine own desire I am
empowered hunger
At your will and call

Napeai babagen ds brin vx ooaona lring vonph doalim,
eolis ollog orsba ds chis affa. Micma isro mad od lonshitox
ds ivmd aai grosb. Zacar od zamran: odo cicle qaa: zorge:
lap zirdo noco mad, hoath iaida

Adgt vpaah zongom faaip sald, viiv l, sobam ialprg izazaz
piadph: casarma abaramg ta talho paracleda, qta lorslq
turbs ooge baltoh. Giui chis lurd orri, od micalp chis bia
ozongon, lap noan trof cors tage, oq manin iaidon. Torzu
gohel: zacar ca cnoqod: zamran micalzo: od ozazm vrelp:
lap zir ioiad.
NEMA! LIVEES, MORF SU REVILLED TUB
NOISHAYTPMET OOTNI TON SUH DEEL SUS
TSHAIGA SAPSERT TAHT YETH. VIGRAWF EU ZA
SESAPSERT RUA SUH VIGRAWF DERB ILAID RUA
YED SITH SUH VIG NEVEH NI SI ZA THRE NI NUD
EEB LIW EYTH MUCK MODNGIK EYTH MAIN
EYTH EEB DWOHLAH NEVAH NI TRA CHIOO.
RETHARF RUA!

Born Again of The Blasphemies
By the Blood Pact
I am your Harvest
Fallen Prey
your desire, your lure
I am Born of the dragon, Harlot, with Unholy Spirit

Sodomize the Children of Abel, that their pleasure gasps
Will enrage your Vengeance Divine
Oh Tasa reme laris Satan, my soul is Thine!!!!!!
Oh Tasa reme laris Satan, my soul is Thine!!!!!!
Oh Tasa reme laris Satan, my soul is Thine!!!!!!
Oh Tasa reme laris Satan, my soul is Thine!!!!!!
Oh Tasa reme laris Satan, my soul is Thine!!!!!!
Oh Tasa reme laris Satan, my soul is Thine!!!!!!
Oh Spirit of Passion, Hate and rebellion come forth in thy smoke
Shemhammforash, Hail Satan, Hail Lianna!!!!!!!!

Prayer for Inner Strength

Tezrian, grant me the wisdom to find my strength. I am transformed in your light. You stand alongside me to face those who oppose me. With you as my guide I will traverse the obstacles that fall in my path. I invoke you as a part of my own inner-strength. May I be blessed with your divine strength. Amen.

For Him

Praise be to Satan, for He leads us from the Darkness and brings us to the light. Praise be to Satan, for He grants us strength and courage. Praise be to Satan, for He rules this world and allows us to indulge in earthly pleasures without guilt or threat of retribution. Praise be to Satan, for He stands up for us as we shall stand up for Him and all He stands for. Bless us, Satan, and show us Your true Nature. Blessed is the Beast, Amen

Blessings

In the name of Satan may you be blessed in the Light of Lucifer. Ave Satana.

By Belial and Leviathan, and in the name of Satan, may this water be blessed. In His name may this seal bring strength and favor upon you/item.

Chosen and blessed in the name of Satan, Amen.

Naamah. (Naamah is a Daemoness of Blessings and it is said her name alone is blessing enough.)

In the name of Satan, and those Daemons who keep order in the earthly domain, Amen.

Blessed be Satan who passes his favor upon you. Amen.

PROVERBS

The following proverbs were found carved on the walls of ancient Egyptian temples. Since many Daemonolaters believe in the Hermetic foundation of our religion, we felt it proper to go back to the source for inspiration. We have included slight modification in some of them for Daemonolaters and Traditional/Theistic Satanists indicated by [ ]. Please note that Maat has been changed to Satan because both deity names represent the same. Heaven (in the sense of kingdom) has been changed to infernal kingdom. Heaven in the sense of enlightenment has been changed to Lucifer. Neter has been left alone. Neter is an Egyptian word for the forces that are god or a group of gods that is the same as the Demonic Divine.

1. The [infernal] kingdom ~~of Heaven~~ is within you; and whosoever shall know himself shall find it.

2. The best and shortest road towards knowledge of truth [is] Nature.

3. For every joy there is a price to be paid.

4. If his heart rules him, his conscience will soon take the place of the rod.

5. What you are doing does not matter so much as what you are learning from doing it.

6. It is better not to know and to know that one does not know, than presumptuously to attribute some random meaning to symbols.

7. If you search for the laws of harmony, you will find knowledge.

8. If you are searching for a Neter, observe Nature!

9. Exuberance is a good stimulus towards action, but the inner light grows in silence and concentration.

10. Not the greatest Master can go even one step for his disciple; in himself he must experience each stage of developing consciousness. Therefore he will know nothing for which he is not ripe.

11. The body is the house of ~~God~~ [the Demonic Divine]. That is why it is said, "Man know thyself."

12. True teaching is not an accumulation of knowledge; it is an awakening of consciousness which goes through successive stages.

13. The man who knows how to lead one of his brothers towards what he has known may one day be saved by that very brother.

14. People bring about their own undoing through their tongues.

15. If one tries to navigate unknown waters one runs the risk of shipwreck. Leave him in error who loves his error.

16. Every man is rich in excuses to safeguard his prejudices, his instincts, and his opinions.

17. To know means to record in one's memory; but to understand means to blend with the thing and to assimilate it oneself.

18. There are two kinds of error: blind credulity and piecemeal criticism.

19. Never believe a word without putting its truth to the test; discernment does not grow in laziness; and this faculty of discernment is indispensable to the Seeker. Sound skepticism is the necessary condition for good discernment; but piecemeal criticism is an error.

20. Love is one thing, knowledge is another.

21. True sages are those who give what they have, without meanness and without secret!

22. An answer brings no illumination unless the question has matured to a point where it gives rise to this answer which thus becomes its fruit. Therefore learn how to put a question.

23. What reveals itself to me ceases to be mysterious for me alone: if I unveil it to anyone else, he hears mere words which betray the living sense: Profanation, but never revelation.

24. The first concerning the 'secrets': all cognition comes from inside; we are therefore initiated only by ourselves, but the Master gives the keys.

25. The second concerning the 'way': the seeker has need of a Master to guide him and lift him up when he falls, to lead him back to the right way when he strays.

26. Understanding develops by degrees.

27. As to deserving, know that the gift of ~~Heaven~~ [Lucifer] is free; this gift of Knowledge is so great that no effort whatever could hope to 'deserve' it.

28. If the Master teaches what is error, the disciple's submission is slavery; if he teaches truth, this submission is ennoblement.

29. There grows no wheat where there is no grain.

30. The only thing that is humiliating is helplessness.

31. An answer is profitable in proportion to the intensity of the quest.

32. Listen to your conviction, even if they seem absurd to your reason.

33. Know the world in yourself. Never look for yourself in the world, for this would be to project your illusion.

34. To teach one must know the nature of those whom one is teaching. In every vital activity it is the path that matters.

35. The way of knowledge is narrow.

36. Each truth you learn will be, for you, as new as if it had never been written.

37. The only active force that arises out of possession is fear of losing the object of possession.

38. If you defy an enemy by doubting his courage you double it.

39. The nut doesn't reveal the tree it contains. For knowledge ... you should know that peace is an indispensable condition of getting it.

40. The first thing necessary in teaching is a master; the second is a pupil capable of carrying on the tradition.

41. Peace is the fruit of activity, not of sleep. Envious greed must govern to possess and ambition must possess to govern.

42. When the governing class isn't chosen for quality it is chosen for material wealth: this always means decadence, the lowest stage a society can reach.

43. Two tendencies govern human choice and effort, the search after quantity and the search after quality. They classify mankind. Some follow Maat [Satan], others seek the way of animal instinct.

44. Qualities of a moral order are measured by deeds.

45. One foot isn't enough to walk with.

46. Our senses serve to affirm, not to know.

47. We mustn't confuse mastery with mimicry, knowledge with superstitious ignorance.

48. Physical consciousness is indispensable for the achievement of knowledge.

49. A man can't be judge of his neighbor's intelligence. His own vital experience is never his neighbor's.

50. No discussion can throw light if it wanders from the real point.

51. Your body is the temple of knowledge.

52. Experience will show you, a Master can only point the way.

53. A house has the character of the man who lives in it.

54. All organs work together in the functioning of the whole.

55. A man's heart is his own Neter.

56. A pupil may show you by his own efforts how much he deserves to learn from you.

57. Routine and prejudice distort vision. Each man thinks his own horizon is the limit of the world.

58. You will free yourself when you learn to be neutral and follow the instructions of your heart without letting things perturb you. This is the way of M̶a̶a̶t̶ [Satan].

59. Judge by cause, not by effect.

60. Growth in consciousness doesn't depend on the will of the intellect or its possibilities but on the intensity of the inner urge.

61. Every man must act in the rhythm of his time ... such is wisdom.

62. Men need images. Lacking them they invent idols. Better then to found the images on realities that lead the true seeker to the source. ~~Maat~~ [Satan], who links universal to terrestrial, the divine with the human is incomprehensible to the cerebral intelligence.

63. Have the wisdom to abandon the values of a time that has passed and pick out the constituents of the future. An environment must be suited to the age and men to their environment.

64. Everyone finds himself in the world where he belongs. The essential thing is to have a fixed point from which to check its reality now and then.

65. Always watch and follow nature.

66. A phenomenon always arises from the interaction of complementaries. If you want something look for the complement that will elicit it. Set causes Horus. Horus redeems Set.

67. All seed answer light, but the color is different. The plant reveals what is in the seed.

68. Popular beliefs on essential matters must be examined in order to discover the original thought.

69. It is the passive resistance from the helm that steers the boat. The key to all problems is the problem of consciousness.

70. Man must learn to increase his sense of responsibility and of the fact that everything he does will have its consequences.

71. If you would build something solid, don't work with wind: always look for a fixed point, something you know that is stable ... yourself.

72. If you would know yourself, take yourself as starting point and go back to its source; your beginning will disclose your end.

73. Images are nearer reality than cold definitions. Seek peacefully, you will find.

74. Organization is impossible unless those who know the laws of harmony lay the foundation.

75. It is no use whatever preaching Wisdom to men: you must inject it into their blood.

76. Knowledge is consciousness of reality. Reality is the sum of the laws that govern nature and of the causes from which they flow.

77. Social good is what brings peace to family and society.

78. Knowledge is not necessarily wisdom.

79. By knowing one reaches belief. By doing one gains conviction. When you know, dare.

80. Altruism is the mark of a superior being.

81. All is within yourself. Know your most inward self and look for what corresponds with it in nature.

82. The seed cannot sprout upwards without simultaneously sending roots into the ground. The seed includes all the possibilities of the tree. ...The seed will develop these possibilities, however, only if it receives corresponding energies from the sky.

83. Grain must return to the earth, die, and decompose for new growth to begin.

84. Man, know thyself ... and thou shalt know the gods.

AL-JILWAH

The Al-Jilwah is the disputed (among many Satanists) scripture of many modern theistic Satanists. Allegedly from the Yezidi tradition, this particular scripture is of questionable origin, but does mark a significant place in modern Satanic Literature. It is included here because many Daemonolaters and Theistic Satanists find strength and comfort within the writings despite its controversial origins. So for those who criticize the Al-Jilwah, view it as simply Satanic Literature and interpret it as metaphor and allegory. I suspect you might find something interesting from that perspective. For others, enjoy it as you always have. Please note that the *I* in this text, is viewed as Satan referring to Himself.

AL-JILWAH (THE REVELATION)

Before all creation this revelation was with Melek □â'ûs, who sent 'Abd □â'ûs to this world that he might separate truth known to his particular people.

This was done, first of all, by means of oral tradition, and afterward by means of this book, Al-Jilwah, which the outsiders may neither read nor behold.

CHAPTER I

I was, am now, and shall have no end. I exercise dominion over all creatures and over the affairs of all who are under the protection of my image. I am ever present to help all who trust in me and call upon me in time of need. There is no place in the universe that knows not my presence. I participate in all the affairs which those who are without call evil because their nature is not such as they approve. Every age has its own manager, who directs affairs according to my decrees. This office is changeable from generation to generation, that the ruler of this world and his chiefs may discharge the duties of their respective offices every one in his own turn. I allow everyone to follow the dictates of his own nature, but he that opposes me will regret it sorely. No god has a right to interfere in my affairs, and I have made it an imperative rule that everyone shall refrain from worshiping all gods. All the books of those who are without are altered by them; and they have declined from them, although they were written by the prophets and the apostles. That there are interpolations is seen in the fact that each sect endeavors to prove that the others are wrong and to destroy their books. To me truth and falsehood are known. When temptation comes, I give my covenant to him that trusts in me. Moreover, I give counsel to the skilled directors, for I have appointed them for periods that are known to me. I remember necessary affairs and execute them in due time. I teach and guide those who follow my instruction. If anyone obey me and conform to my commandments, he shall have joy, delight, and goodness.

CHAPTER II

I requite the descendents of Adam, and reward them with various rewards that I alone know. Moreover, power and dominion over all that is on earth, both that which is above and that which is beneath, are in my hand. I do not allow friendly association with other people, nor do I deprive them that are my own and that obey me of anything that is good for them. I place my affairs in the hands of those whom I have tried and who are in accord with my desires. I appear in divers manners to those who are faithful and under my command. I give and take away; I enrich and impoverish; I cause both happiness and misery. I do all this in keeping with the characteristics of each epoch. And none has a right to interfere with my management of affairs. Those who oppose me I afflict with disease; but my own shall not die like the sons of Adam that are without. None shall live in this world longer than the time set by me; and if I so desire, I send a person a second or a third time into this world or into some other by the transmigration of souls.

CHAPTER III

I lead to the straight path without a revealed book; I direct aright my beloved and my chosen ones by unseen means. All my teachings are easily applicable to all times and all conditions. I punish in another world all who do contrary to my will. Now the sons of Adam do not know the state of things that is to come. For this reason they fall into many errors. The beasts of the earth, the birds of heaven, and the fish of the sea are all under the control of my hands. All treasures and hidden things are known to me; and as I desire, I take them from one and bestow them upon another. I reveal my wonders to those who seek them, and, in due time my miracles to those who receive them from me. But those who are without are my adversaries, hence they oppose me. Nor do they know that such a course is against their own interests, for might, wealth, and riches are in my hand, and I bestow them upon every worthy descendant of Adam. Thus the government of the worlds, the transition of generations, and the changes of their directors are determined by me from the beginning.

CHAPTER IV

I will not give my rights to other gods. I have allowed the creation of four substances, four times, and four comers; because they are necessary things for creatures. The books of Jews, Christians, and Moslems, as of those who are without, accept in a sense, *i.e.*, so far as they agree with, and conform to, my statutes. Whatsoever is contrary to these they have altered; do not accept it. Three things are against me, and I hate three things. But those who keep my secrets shall receive the fulfillment of my promises. Those who suffer for my sake I will surely reward in one of the worlds. It is my desire that all my followers shall unite in a bond of unity, lest those who are without prevail against them. Now, then, all ye who have followed my commandments and my teachings, reject all the teachings and sayings of such as are without. I have not taught these teachings, nor do they proceed from me. Do not mention my name nor my attributes, lest ye regret it; for ye do not know what those who are without may do.

CHAPTER V

O ye that have believed in me, honor my symbol and my image, for they remind you of me. Observe my laws and statutes. Obey my servants and listen to whatever they may dictate to you of the hidden things. Receive that that is dictated, and do not carry it before those who are without, Jews, Christians, Moslems, and others; for they know not the nature of my teaching. Do not give them your books, lest they alter them without your knowledge. Learn by heart the greater part of them, lest they be altered.

Thus endeth the book of Al-Jilwah, which is followed by the book of Ma□ □af Reš, *i.e.*, the Black Book.

A Demonolatry and Literary Perspective of the Al-Jilwah
By S. Connolly

This commentary was actually written for another project, however, since I own the rights to this essay, I thought I would include it in the prayer/scripture book as insight for those Demonoaltors looking at the Al-Jilwah and wondering why it was included.

When it comes to the Al-Jilwah of the Yezidis, the seasoned occult scholar can immediately and clearly define the roles of Demons, although differently named, in the Yezidis tradition. The Yezidis is a small sect comprised of approximately 200,000 followers. Like many Demonolatry sect traditions, the Yezidis pass their faith to each subsequent generation. This tradition has been passed orally. The sect was studied extensively in the late 19th and early 20th century by theologians from across the globe, who found interesting similarities to Christianity within the religious *structure* of the sect. Some speculate the sect is much older than Christianity and conformed some of its original traditions to the mold of the Christian ways in order that they might survive the Christian onset. Aside from Christian tradition there are also traces of Muslim and Persian influence. There are nine positive influence "arch-angels" or "Demonic entities" worshipped by the Yezidis.

While there is little documentation of true Demonolatry sects in history, the Yezidis, although obscure and not necessarily considered Demonolaters by all, remain the best-documented and researched Demonolatry sect of all time outside the Western Demonolatry community. That is, of course, if you believe the Yezidis comprise a valid Demonolatry sect.

There is a lot of controversy among Demonolaters regarding the validity of such claims since, when shown copies of the translated Al Jilwah and the "Black Book", some Yezidis priests were amused, while others were offended. It is really unclear whether the Yezidis are actually worshiping angels or demons or even Satan as many Westerners think. In recent years, the Al-Jilwah has become a prominent text in the modern Theistic and Traditional Satanism movement, but has still not become a text of influence for many Demonolaters simply because of its somewhat Abrahamic overtones (mainly deity having human shortcomings and there being a war against good and evil with man as the warrior pawns in the middle). Others, however, have found it a scripture of some personal significance and have found strength and comfort in the text's literary allusion and metaphor.

Once you take the text out of its alleged historical context and view it as simply a piece of influential Satanic literature, the Al Jilwah takes on a life of its own and gives a subtle message of strength and lessons to live by for all who dare tread the darker path. Personally, as a Daemonolatress, I do not view the text of the Al Jilwah historically or literally or from an Abrahamic viewpoint. Instead, I look at it and see a piece of controversial literature that hides a fascinating perspective.

The following is my personal interpretation of the Al-Jilwah as Satanic literature from a Demonolater's perspective.

CHAPTER I

I was, am now, and shall have no end. I exercise dominion over all creatures and over the affairs of all who are under the protection of my image. I am ever present to help all who trust in me and call upon me in time of need. There is no place in the universe that knows not my presence. I participate in all the affairs which those who are without call evil because their nature is not such as they approve. Every age has its own manager, who directs affairs according to my decrees. This office is changeable from generation to generation, that the ruler of this world and his chiefs may discharge the duties of their respective offices every one in his own turn. I allow everyone to follow the dictates of his own nature, but he that opposes me will regret it sorely. No god has a right to interfere in my affairs, and I have made it an imperative rule that everyone shall refrain from worshiping all gods. All the books of those who are without are altered by them; and they have declined from them, although they were written by the prophets and the apostles. That there are interpolations is seen in the fact that each sect endeavors to prove that the others are wrong and to destroy their books. To me truth and falsehood are known. When temptation comes, I give my covenant to him that trusts in me. Moreover, I give counsel to the skilled directors, for I have appointed them for periods that are known to me. I remember necessary affairs and execute them in due time. I teach and guide those who follow my instruction. If anyone obey me and conform to my commandments, he shall have joy, delight, and goodness.

The first chapter is not the description of a "God" necessarily. Instead, it describes the All of Creation. The Ether of All that Is, He that we Satanists and Demonolaters call, Satan. Basically it suggests that those who will never know the nature of Satan are without (i.e. ignorant). Not because there is a war between Abrahamic religions and "others" but rather because religion such as the Abrahamic triad of faiths, separates us from the spirit, and the source of our creation which is Satan. Those who are with, on the path of Satan, are joined with the source of all that is, and will grow in its infernal light. This also suggests one Deity above all others. While I view the wording as the author arrogantly anthropomorphizing deity (again), I also see it suggesting that all Gods are part of the One. They all must bow down to the one. This is a basic Hermetic concept regarding the source ruling over everything, including lower gods and all parts of the Whole. With regards to the passage, "...and I have made it an imperative rule that everyone shall refrain from worshiping all gods." I view this line as not seeing the Gods as being above the All. Of course literally it suggests that Satan is judgmental and has human faults, which I don't agree with. So I think that line is simply in support of soft Polytheism (from a metaphoric perspective, of course).

CHAPTER II

I requite the descendents of Adam, and reward them with various rewards that I alone know. Moreover, power and dominion over all that is on earth, both that which is above and that which is beneath, are in my hand. I do not allow friendly association with other people, nor do I deprive them that are my own and that obey me of anything that is good for them. I place my affairs in the hands of those whom I have tried and who are in accord with my desires. I appear in divers manners to those who are faithful and under my command. I give and take away; I enrich and impoverish; I cause both happiness and misery. I do all this in keeping with the characteristics of each epoch. And none has a right to interfere with my management of affairs. Those who oppose me I afflict with disease; but my own shall not die like the sons of Adam that are without. None shall live in this world longer than the time set by me; and if I so desire, I send a person a second or a third time into this world or into some other by the transmigration of souls.

Obviously descendents of Adam is a metaphor for humans. I am unsure why the author of this text chose an Abrahamic metaphor to describe mankind. My only thought on this is the possibility that perhaps Adam comes from Atem or Atum, as we were considered children of Atem by the Ancient Egyptians, who also held the philosophies that the Gods and Man all came from the same source and that source was the source of All, Atem (also Satan). I, like many Demonolaters, believe that most of Abrahamic myth, prayer, ritual, etc... was taken from ancient cultures (Egypt and Sumeria). The second chapter really focuses on balance, duality, and polarity, much like the Hermetic principle of polarity. It also suggests universal consciousness and pre-destination, that life is cyclic, which we know to be true.

CHAPTER III

I lead to the straight path without a revealed book; I direct aright my beloved and my chosen ones by unseen means. All my teachings are easily applicable to all times and all conditions. I punish in another world all who do contrary to my will. Now the sons of Adam do not know the state of things that is to come. For this reason they fall into many errors. The beasts of the earth, the birds of heaven, and the fish of the sea are all under the control of my hands. All treasures and hidden things are known to me; and as I desire, I take them from one and bestow them upon another. I reveal my wonders to those who seek them, and, in due time my miracles to those who receive them from me. But those who are without are my adversaries, hence they oppose me. Nor do they know that such a course is against their own interests, for might, wealth, and riches are in my hand, and I bestow them upon every worthy descendant of Adam. Thus the government of the worlds, the transition of generations, and the changes of their directors are determined by me from the beginning.

"Teachings" for "all times and conditions", and the control of all living things, suggests to me the natural laws. This entire chapter simply defines the nature of Satan as a natural part of the universe.

CHAPTER IV
I will not give my rights to other gods. I have allowed the creation of four substances, four times, and four comers; because they are necessary things for creatures. The books of Jews, Christians, and Moslems, as of those who are without, accept in a sense, *i.e.*, so far as they agree with, and conform to, my statutes. Whatsoever is contrary to these they have altered; do not accept it. Three things are against me, and I hate three things. But those who keep my secrets shall receive the fulfillment of my promises. Those who suffer for my sake I will surely reward in one of the worlds. It is my desire that all my followers shall unite in a bond of unity, lest those who are without prevail against them. Now, then, all ye who have followed my commandments and my teachings, reject all the teachings and sayings of such as are without. I have not taught these teachings, nor do they proceed from me. Do not mention my name nor my attributes, lest ye regret it; for ye do not know what those who are without may do.

"Four Substances, Four Times, and Four Corners", from my perspective, obviously refers to the elements because they're all necessary for life. We require air to breathe, and water to drink, and the earth for our food, and lastly, fire for warmth and helping life to flourish. By saying that man cannot go against Satan, this is not like upsetting your Dad, but rather causing irreparable damage to the universe itself or the nature sustaining us (global warming comes to mind) that will cause our own demise (punishment for ruining nature and that which sustains our own lives). This could also be viewed as eating poorly, or smoking, or doing something bad for your health (unnatural) causing your own death (hence punishment). This is basically saying your body, your planet, and your universe is your temple. Treat all of them with care or risk destroying yourself.

CHAPTER V

O ye that have believed in me, honor my symbol and my image, for they remind you of me. Observe my laws and statutes. Obey my servants and listen to whatever they may dictate to you of the hidden things. Receive that that is dictated, and do not carry it before those who are without, Jews, Christians, Moslems, and others; for they know not the nature of my teaching. Do not give them your books, lest they alter them without your knowledge. Learn by heart the greater part of them, lest they be altered.

The servants are the Demons from my perspective. The Demonic Divine who teach the wisdom of Satan's natural laws and guide us through our physical lives and on to the next plane of existence. The latter sentences simply say that none of this can be written down. True understanding comes from within because all books (even this one) can be rewritten to mean something else or interpreted in a number of ways, hiding the true wisdom and knowledge. True wisdom and knowledge, as the Egyptians pointed out, is not something that can be memorized and spat out. True wisdom and knowledge comes from experience.

I think much of the Al-Jilwah seems anti-Abrahamic in general. Not because of a war between "good and evil". Basically I think it means that the minute we show the nature of the universe to those who don't get it (certain groups of Christians, for example) - they're going to deny it and try to suppress it like they have done with certain scientific discoveries, stem cells, global warming, and evolution to name a few. All of these natural things - when presented to certain institutions of Christianity (or other Abrahamic faith), have caused conflict. I kind of look at all of the statements suggesting we separate ourselves from Abrahamic religion as "Don't talk to the brick wall because you're wasting your breath."

And this, my brethren, is how I interpret the positive and hopeful message of the Al-Jilwah from a Demonolatry and Literary perspective. Satan and Lucifer Bless.

Made in the USA
Monee, IL
08 October 2021